THE CANADIAN
ROCKIES

WHITECAP BOOKS
VANCOUVER / TORONTO

Text by Tanya Lloyd

Edited by Elaine Jones

Proofread by Lisa Collins

Cover and interior design by Steve Penner

Photo editing by Pat Crowe

Desktop publishing by Susan Greenshields

Printed and bound in Canada

Canadian Cataloguing in Publication Data

Lloyd, Tanya, 1973–

    The Canadian Rockies

    (Canada series)
    ISBN 1-55110-930-1

1. Rocky Mountains, Canadian (B.C. and Alta.)--Pictorial works.*
I. Title. II. Series: Canada series (North Vancouver, B.C.)
FC219.L59 1999   971.1'0022'2   C99-910261-3
F1090.L56 1999

The publisher acknowledges the support of the Canada Council and the Cultural Services Branch of the Government of British Columbia in making this publication possible. We acknowledge the financial support of the Government of Canada through the Book Publishing Industry Development Program for our publishing activities.

For more information on the Canada Series and other Whitecap Books titles, please visit our web site at www.whitecap.ca.

istorian Virgil Martin once wrote "If a globe were to be made 12 inches (30 cm) in diameter, with every detail of the earth's surface reproduced exactly to scale, the highest mountain in the Canadian Rockies would be represented by a bump roughly equal to the thickness of a single leaf of this book." That may be so, but the Rocky Mountains loom much larger in the Canadian imagination. They are the symbol of the western frontier. They boast Banff, the country's first and most renowned national park. They are home to many of the animals—moose, wolves, bears, and elk—that we associate with the Canadian wilderness.

The rugged peaks and emerald lakes of the Rocky Mountains not only dominate the geography of British Columbia and Alberta, but affect the landscapes of the continent as well. From the Columbia Icefield, meltwater feeds the Fraser and Columbia rivers, which run into the Pacific; it swells the Saskatchewan River system, which empties into the Atlantic; and it leads into the Mackenzie River, surging towards the Arctic ocean.

For centuries, the mountains formed a formidable barrier to trade and communication. The breaching of this barrier by the Canadian Pacific Railway in the late 1800s irrevocably changed the development of the region and the nation. Among other changes was a rapid growth in tourism, a trend that continues today. The creation of a 26-square-kilometre (10-square-mile) park by the Canadian government in 1885 was the starting point for more than 36 national parks, the largest federal park system in the world. And the explorations of railway workers, amateur geologists, outfitters, and guides led to the creation of thousands of kilometres of hiking trails, giving access to some of Canada's most spectacular sights. The photographers featured in this book have hiked some of these trails, capturing images of the remote alpine, as well as the familiar scenes—Peyto Lake, Mount Robson, Takakkaw Falls—that epitomize this range.

Vermilion Lakes is a favourite with visitors, in part for its spectacular views of Mount Rundle. This is also an excellent bird-watching venue. Migrating birds, such as swans, mergansers, and grebes, find the lakes a tempting resting place.

6

Rushing meltwater has carved narrow canyons throughout the Rockies. A walking path in Johnston Canyon, along the Bow Valley Parkway, leads visitors past seven waterfalls within the gorge.

OPPOSITE —
A trail up Tunnel Mountain, offering a panoramic view of Mount Rundle, is a popular day hike in Banff National Park. This pristine scenery remains protected under the National Parks Act of 1930, which dedicated the land to the people of Canada "for their benefit, education, and enjoyment."

Geologist A. P. Coleman was one of the first to take the Canadian Pacific Railway to the Rockies. When he arrived in 1884, he wrote, "After years of humdrum city life...here was purity and dignity and measureless peace."

A snow-cloaked road leads to Lake Minnewanka,
the largest lake in Banff National Park.

Picturesque Bow Lake lies in a gentle alpine bowl beneath the peak of Crowfoot Glacier. This glacier offers one of the most accessible ice cliffs in the Rockies.

The Weeping Wall is named for the waterfalls that cascade over this limestone cliff, creating curtains of ice each winter.

14

Bow Falls near the Banff Springs Hotel feed Bow River
and, in turn, the South Saskatchewan River system.

Banff has a population of only 7,500, but millions of visitors flock to the town each year to shop at the exclusive boutiques, dine at the wide variety of cafés and restaurants, or simply enjoy the scenery.

Founded in 1885, Banff is the oldest national park in North America, with the exception of Yellowstone, set aside in 1872.

Banff Hot Springs were the first of several in the Rockies to be developed and advertised to the public. The original facility, opened in 1914, housed what was then the world's largest swimming pool.

OPPOSITE —
When it was completed in 1888, Banff Springs Hotel was the largest in the world. It now boasts 788 rooms and offers guests golf, tennis, bowling, spa facilities, a disco, and more than 40 shops.

Wrangler Tom Wilson, working for the Canadian Pacific Railway, became the first European to see Lake Louise in 1882. He named it Emerald Lake, but renamed it Lake Louise two years later.

Snow cloaks a cabin on the shore of Lake Louise. Some say the lake was named in honour of Louise Temple, whose father was Sir Richard Temple of the British Association for the Advancement of Science. However, most believe it was named for Princess Louise Caroline Alberta, daughter of Queen Victoria.

Chateau Lake Louise could host twelve guests when it opened in 1892. It now offers almost 500 rooms, with some of the best views in the world.

The lynx hunts the forests of the Rockies for snowshoe hare, its primary prey. This wildcat must be persistent to feed her young— she will succeed in only 15 of every 100 attempts to capture the hare.

Hikers can follow a trail through Larch Valley up to the Wenkchemna Peaks, a route that explorer Walter Wilcox called "possibly the most spectacular and inspiring in the mountains."

25

Peyto Lake was reputedly one of the favourite camping sites of Bill Peyto, a British-born outfitter whose knowledge of the Rockies made him one of the area's most respected guides.

With wood-burning fireplaces, a pool, a whirlpool, a sauna,
and an array of dining choices, the Post Hotel offers elegant
accommodations to Lake Louise visitors.

One glance at the formidable ramparts of Castle
Mountain explains its name. After the Second
World War, this mountain was temporarily known
as Mount Eisenhower. One of the peaks still
bears the name of the American president.

Bighorn sheep grow a new ring on their curled horns each year. These agile creatures thrive on the steep cliffs and in the alpine meadows of the Rockies.

Explorer Walter Wilcox named Moraine Lake in 1893, believing the debris at one end of the lake was a moraine left by a glacier. Geologists now believe it is the remains of a rock slide from the peak above.

The Columbia
Icefield between
Mount Columbia and
Mount Athabasca is
up to 365 metres
(1200 feet) deep in
places. The largest
icefield south of
the Arctic Circle,
it encompasses
about 30 glaciers.

The Columbia Icefield Chalet stands near the base of the glaciers,
offering unique accommodation for some of the thousands
of visitors who flock to the icefield each year.

Wilcox Pass is named for Walter Wilcox, a Yale College student, photographer, and amateur geologist who explored the Rockies in the late 19th century. Wilcox was one of the first non-natives to see Moraine Lake, the Valley of the Ten Peaks, Paradise Valley, and other natural wonders of the range.

Jasper National Park was established to attract railway passengers in the early 1900s. It was named after Jasper Hawes, the manager of a nearby fur-trading post.

Lower Waterfowl Lake is just one of the magnificent views glimpsed by travellers on the Icefield Parkway, a 230-kilometre (140-mile) drive between Banff and Jasper.

In 1979, Alpine Club of Canada member Don Forest became the first person to reach the summits of all peaks in the Canadian Rockies over 3400 metres (1100 feet). One of these peaks was Mount Athabasca, which rises to 3940 metres (12,930 feet).

Of Jasper National Park's 10,800 square kilometres (4200 square miles), only about 10 percent is valley bottom. The rest is a combination of jagged peaks and alpine passes.

Jasper Park Lodge was built by the Canadian National Railway in 1922. It was designed to compete with Banff Springs Hotel to the south, on the CPR's more established route.

Angel Glacier glistens on the slopes of Mount Edith Cavell.
Originally known as Mount Fitzhugh, the peak was renamed
in 1916 in honour of a British nurse. Cavell was shot in 1915
after helping Allied soldiers escape German territory.

The unique cliffs of the Ramparts make the mountain one of the most recognizable in Jasper National Park, and one of the most photographed peaks in the Rockies.

Maligne Lake, the largest in the Canadian Rockies, stretches for 22 kilometres. In 1908, the first non-native to discover it was Mary Shaffer, a widow from Philadelphia who spent her summers in the mountains.

Known as wapiti, elk are a common sight in the remote meadows and along roadsides in Banff and Jasper national parks. Hikers may hear their distinctive, high-pitched calls in the evenings.

Silt in the glacial water is slowly eroding the cliff beneath Athabasca Falls. Many of the waterfalls in the Rockies are becoming steadily lower.

Maligne Canyon is connected to a large network of caves. It is possible that the canyon was formed when erosion caused the roofs of some caves to collapse.

50

Willmore Wilderness
Park was named for
Norman Willmore, a
former Alberta minister of
lands and forests. The park
is a favourite destination
for backpackers and
horseback riders.

OPPOSITE —
The largest provincial park
in the Rockies, Willmore
Wilderness Park is also
one of the least accessible.

Created as a
recreational area
by the Alberta
government in 1977,
Kananaskis Country
includes several
distinct ecosystems,
from aspen groves
and dry grasslands
to rugged foothills
and towering peaks.

55

A helicopter hovers over the front ranges of the Rockies in Kananaskis Country. The 4250-square-kilometre (1640-square-mile) preserve includes three provincial parks: Peter Lougheed, Bow Valley, and Bragg Creek.

Designed in 1983 by Robert Trent Jones Sr., the 36-hole Kananaskis Country Golf Course draws visitors from around the world.

Mount Assiniboine, 3618 metres (11,870 feet) high, has been called the Matterhorn of the Canadian Rockies.

A group of grizzlies fishing a fast-moving mountain stream are easily identifiable by their distinctive humps. Reports of grizzlies in the Rockies vary, but there may be up to 2,000.

Tourism boomed in the Rockies with the arrival of the railroad. William Cornelius Van Horne, vice-president of the Canadian Pacific Railway at the turn of the century, is known for his words, "If we can't export the scenery, we'll import the tourists."

The nodding heads of glacier lilies can be found throughout the mountains, sometimes just a few steps away from the snowline.

Explorer and guide Kootenai Brown was instrumental in the creation of Waterton Lakes National Park and served as its first superintendent. It was Brown, along with Glacier National Park ranger Henry Reynolds, who proposed an international reserve.

Built by the American company Great Northern Railroad to serve its passengers, the Prince of Wales Hotel is the largest wood-framed building in Alberta.

Waterton Lakes National Park in Alberta and Glacier National Park in Montana together form Waterton-Glacier International Peace Park. The preserve was created in 1932 and was the first park of its kind in the world.

Red Rock Canyon in Waterton Lakes National Park was part of an ancient sea. The iron in the rocks oxidized as the sea evaporated, leaving layers of minerals behind.

The peaks of the Three Sisters near Canmore mark the gateway
between Banff National Park and Kananaskis Country.

Home to 8,000 people, the town of Canmore
offers access to hiking, skiing, and mountaineering
in the surrounding mountains.

Backcountry skiers explore the steep slopes and pristine basins of the mountains near Canmore.

Tiny particles of glacier-ground silt suspended in Emerald Lake lend the lake its distinctive colour. Visitors can explore these waters by canoe or walk an interpretive trail around the lake.

Just moments away from the Trans-Canada Highway, Emerald Lake is one of the most accessible glacier-fed lakes in the Rockies. The first road reached this area in 1928.

The rushing currents of Kicking Horse River have slowly worn
a tunnel through the rock bank, creating this natural bridge.

The movement of the earth's crust transported
fossils from an ancient sea high into the
mountains, forming what is now known
as the Burgess Shale. The area was declared
a UNESCO World Heritage Site in 1980.

Yoho is derived from a Cree word meaning "awe." The stunning natural scenery of Yoho National Park attracts about 700,000 visitors each year.

Within the 1310 square kilometres (505 square miles) of Yoho National Park, there are 28 peaks over 3000 metres (9850 feet) high.

OPPOSITE —
There are more than 600 plant species within Yoho National Park. Some, like this fireweed, thrive in even the harshest alpine conditions.

A short loop trail from
Lake O'Hara leads hikers to
the Opabin Plateau, a small
valley filled with streams,
ponds, and lush meadows.

OPPOSITE —
Meltwater from the
Daly Glacier and
Waputik Icefield plunges
384 metres (1260 feet)
at Takakkaw Falls,
British Columbia's
second-highest waterfall.

Downhill skiers
slice through powder
on the slopes near
Valemount, B.C.

The squirrel's skill at collecting food in summer and fall—from nuts and seeds to insects and mushrooms—keeps it well fed in winter. Squirrels may tunnel through deep snow to reach their stockpiles.

Explorers Dr. Cheadle and Lord Milton glimpsed the peak of Mount Robson, usually obscured by cloud, in 1863. They called it "a giant among giants, and immeasurably supreme." Mount Robson Provincial Park was established in 1913.

The Vermilion Range connects Kootenay National Park with Banff. Unfortunately, about 2440 hectares (6030 acres) of the Vermilion River Valley was destroyed by fire in 1968.

Jagged rock formations dominate the cliffs of Sinclair Canyon, in Kootenay National Park.

Native people once used the ochre-coloured clay in the Paint Pots of Kootenay National Park for body decorating, rock painting, and leather dying. The colour is caused by a high concentration of iron in the underground springs.

The Rockwall, in Kootenay National Park, is a 600-metre (1970-foot) lime-stone cliff that drops dramatically to the waters of Floe Lake.

Travelling in packs of up to 20 animals, wolves can roam more than 30 kilometres (19 miles) in a single day. Keen senses—wolves can hear noises more than two kilometres (one mile) away—help them avoid contact with humans.

Kootenay National Park was established in 1920. The land for the park was ceded by the provincial government in exchange for the construction of the Banff-Windermere road through the mountains.

Photo Credits